The Wind is Blowing a Hooligan

by

David Agnew

Earthspot Books,
9 Normanby Terrace, Flat 1, Whitby, YO21 3ES, UK.

ISBN 978-1-898728-40-5

2 3 4 5 6 7 8 9

Contents

Acknowledgements

Thanks are due to the members of the Whitby Writers Group and its Poetry Group offshoot, whose sympathetic feedback and encouragement led to significant improvement in many of the poems.

The following poems were included in *Love The Words,* broadcast by Chapel FM on 21st June 2016…

Knowledge
Facts of Life N° 126
Every Seventh is a Big One
Ownership
The Wind is Blowing a Hooligan
Debonair
Reach Out

They are available as audio podcasts on their website: www.chapelfm.co.uk

Introduction

David Agnew was born in Northern Ireland, 1944, and currently, having fulfilled one of his dreams, lives in Whitby. He has been writing poetry for more than a decade and his poems have appeared in a variety of magazines and anthologies.

His acclaimed first collection *Walking into Eternity* (Flux Gallery Press 2006) was followed by the book-length prose poem *First I Dreamt the Journey* (2008) and his well-respected *There Are No Such Things As Seagulls* (Valley Press 2012), which explored his love of Whitby despite living elsewhere.

Having moved to live in Whitby in early 2015 this book collects together poems written since he moved, with the poems presented in the order they were written as this too tells a story.

More of his poetry can be found on his Facebook page.

Knowledge

We walked along the prom.
You held my hand,
were enamoured
by everything Whitby,
were delighted for me
that I had found
a place where I was content.

We went to the Magpie
for fish and chips,
essential I think
on your first
visit to Whitby.

Later, back at my flat,
as we watched and listened
to the gulls, we both knew
we would do
this again.

Early Morning

I sit here in my armchair,
mug of tea in hand,
and work my way
gently into the day.

I scroll through
messages on my phone,
they make me feel warm,
give me a glow,
which I can carry
through the rest of my day.

So I open the window,
recline my chair,
listen to the gulls,
reflect.
The rest of the day
can wait until
a little bit later.

The Now

We stepped sideways,
I think,
through a portal
in the firmament
into a different space,

where time,
it seemed,
stood still
and everything
was in the now.

Photography

"Am I a photographer?" I ask myself
as I stand on the pier, camera in hand.
"No" I reply "I am a poet,
I paint pictures with words."

But taking my camera
causes me to stop, causes me to look.
Hockney says "if you look long enough
and hard enough you will see
the colours which are there."

So I do look long enough,
do look hard enough,
take the occasional picture.

But really it is all about
the just being there,
the losing myself
in that looking
and the existing
In that moment.

Across the Bridge

As I assimilate myself
into the mores of Whitby
I become aware
of an East side/West side schism.

A legacy I understand
of the days when
the ships' captains and owners
lived on the West side
and the workers on the East.

And yet it still persists today.
I myself would appear
to perpetuate this custom
for I mostly stay on my own side.

But today I cross the bridge,
go visit Tony's
for a haircut and a chat,
call in, shake hands
with my namesake
at the Humble Pie and Mash.
(How strange for there to be
two of us in a town this size.)

Drop into Jane's
for my breakfast.

Climb the 199 steps?
Ah, for that
I shall cross
the bridge again
another time.

Birthday Dilemma

For my birthday she bought me
a shirt, a tie and a jumper,
hung them on one hanger,
said "Always wear them together."

So I wore them to a party
held by other friends.
Their twenty-something daughter,
never known for her tact,
said "For someone who
doesn't do colour-co-ordination
that is pretty impressive."

Should I confess?

Plans

If you want
to give God
a laugh
it is said
tell Him your plans.

So I told Him
my plans,
talked about
possibilities
and impossibilities.

Impossibilities
are what He delivered,
each of which
surprised
and delighted me.

I love it when a plan
comes together
but it is probably best
I leave Him
to make the plans.

The Wisdom of Gulls

There is a chill wind blowing,
rain is skittering
across the landscape.

I open the window,
listen to the gulls
who speak to me kindly.

"Today, David, you would be best
staying wrapped up indoors;
PJs and dressing gown will suffice.
Make today a PJs day."

Sounds like a plan to me.

It is All Your Fault

"It is all your fault"
she said
but there was a smile
on her face
as she said it.

"It is all your fault"
has cropped up
in my life before.
At one stage
I thought it must
be written on
my birth certificate.

But there is a difference
between said with love
and said with hate.
I have learned to tell
the difference.

"I didn't say it was all your fault,
I said I was going to blame you."
And she said that too
with a smile on her face.

Call Centre

I spoke to a young man
at the Call Centre
of the company
which supplies my electricity.

Turns out he was born
in the same hospital I was,
for the call centre is based
in my original home town.

All the staff there are pleasant,
friendly and helpful.
Which is just as well really
given the number of times I ring
because of their sheer bloody
incompetence in most other areas.

Not a Choice Really

I could sit on my sofa
in the corner of the room,
turn on the television,
watch whatever's on the box.

Or I could sit in my armchair,
across from an open window,
watch and listen to the birds
go about their daily business.

Poem Written on a Napkin

I sit with a coffee
beside an open door,
watch a soft gentle rain
gradually dampen
the landscape, cleanse the air.

But the rain persists.
I am forced to succumb
to a second coffee
with a large portion
of raspberry, vanilla
and white chocolate cake.

Delicious, just don't tell
my doctor or my son.

Life is a Dangerous Place

I sit in my armchair
with morning mug of tea
gently working towards
the start of a new day.

When suddenly
two seagulls, fighting,
fall off the roof,
land on my patio,
bounce onto the lawn,
carry on fighting.

I am left to ponder
the chances of having
two seagulls, fighting,
landing on my head.

Vitalstatistix

Having introduced onto
my list of anxieties
the fear of seagulls
landing on my head

I find myself drawn
to a comparison
with the chief of the village
in the Asterix stories.

His name – Vitalstatistix
and he was afraid
of nothing other than
the sky would fall on his head.

What is this Multi-tasking?

I do not understand
even the concept
of multi-tasking.

I am a serial person.
I make lists,
do things in sequence,
don't start the next task
until the previous
one is finished.

That is how the bad days
are dealt with,
tick things off the list
and thus get through the day.

Sometimes things do not get done
but I can always
leave them on the list,
do them tomorrow.

Some things have been on
my list for over six months
but as long as they are there
I will get to them eventually.

Or maybe not, perhaps
they will just, in time,
drop off the list.

A Civilised Life

It seems to me to be
remarkably civilised
to go up for my morning paper,
take it next door
to the Windy Corner tea room
and read it accompanied
by a pot of tea and a scone,
or a toasted teacake,
with oodles of butter and jam.
Even if the only part worth reading
is the sports pages.

It seems to me to be
remarkably civilised,
when I decide I cannot
be bothered making lunch,
to go up to the Windy Corner tea room
and have one of a variety
of home made savouries,
with or without fries.
Another day I do not have to cook.

It seems to me to be
remarkably civilised,
after a morning spent in Whitby,
rather than make a cup of tea for one,
to go up to the Windy Corner tea room,
have the tea made for me,
share good company
and admire the home made
cakes on display. Sometimes

Carol will cut me a little
piece just to taste.
There is no sugar in
a little piece just to taste.

Beckett's Coffee Shop

It is really hard, is it not,
when you are not supposed to eat sugar
to sit in Beckett's coffee shop,
with an excellent mug of coffee
and look at the cakes on display –

Chocolate coffee Rolo cake,
Raspberry, white chocolate and vanilla cake,
More-ish chocolate mint swirl,
Summer berry bonanza,
Bertie Bassets bonanza,
Orange and ginger cake,
Gooey mocha swirl,
Dark chocolate and black cherry cake.

See, you are drooling already
yet all you are doing
is reading a poem.

The Real Truth

I was talking
to a young man
in a coffee shop in Whitby.

He was equipped
with the latest smart phone,
showed me its capabilities,
keen to impress me
with how much he knew,
with how wise he was,
with all that data
at his fingertips.

But I could only smile ruefully
as he walked away
for he was totally unaware
of the real truth –

that information is not knowledge
and knowledge is not wisdom.

Facts of Life Nº 126

Pondering on things I need,
things I have to buy,
it occurs to me
that if a woman
is looking for
a man who is single

she could do worse
than loiter in
the men's underwear section
at Marks and Spencer's

for if a man is buying
his own underwear
it is almost certain
he is single.

Wisdom Comes With Age

I stand on the pavement
waiting for a bus
which is late.

I could pace up and down,
get angry, get upset,
but I cannot be arsed.

For it would seem futile
to give control
of my emotions
over to an inanimate
object like a bus.

17 Haikus – Whitby

The gulls, they squabble
noisily on the rooftops
when I leave the house.

Catch the bus to town,
I may well be the youngest
person on the bus.

Does this say something
about longevity
of life in Whitby.

Make a visit to
my favourite coffee shop.
contemplate some cake.

Satisfy myself
instead by toasted teacake
with too much butter.

Get involved in talk
re walks in Whitby for those
of us who struggle.

We all agree that
the cliff lift up from the beach
is a real bonus.

Call in another
shop where they provide a seat
for customer use.

They do not object
when I drop in for only
a rest and a chat.

It is high tide when
I arrive at the swing bridge,
stand awhile to watch.

The whole process of
opening and closing has
me fascinated.

Walk down the harbour,
inspect the boats, then past the
bandstand to the pier.

Find an empty bench,
watch the gulls, watch the waves, but
mostly people watch.

Walk to the very
end of the pier, remember
someone I kissed there.

Climb the steps up to
Captain Cook, on to Clara's
for a strong coffee.

And a seat from where
I can watch the sun as it
sets into the sea.

The gulls still squabble
noisily on the roof tops
when I return home.

Brief Encounter

On a cross-country train
I begin to chat
to a young student from South Wales,
studying medicine she said,

but interested enough in poetry
to key my details into her mobile phone
and look me up on the Internet.

She turned the phone toward me,
said "That is you."
I smile, say yes, but wonder

if I am more real for her now
than I was when
we were just sitting talking.

Then and Now

I sometimes think
'bout then and now
and how I got
from there to here.

Looking back the taken path
is none too clear.
Most days it seems
all I did
was muddle through.

But one thing stands out,
that once I stopped
pouring alcohol
on a whole load of issues
I could find a way.

One simple decision
taken then and taken
daily ever since
has given me
twenty seven years
of added life.

So, just for today,
I will not have a drink.

Every Seventh is a Big One

I am sat on a bench
looking out to sea.
T-shirt weather today,
yesterday was winter.

I am counting waves
for someone told me
every seventh
is a big one.

The evidence so far
is inconclusive.
I may well
be here for hours.

Morning Pages

I awaken early morning,
too soon perhaps to rise.
I would like to lay awhile.

But it is in
those early mornings,
not quite asleep,
not quite awake,
that the dark thoughts appear.

Doors, long since shut tight,
creak open, just enough,
to let the demons out.

They speak of doubt, uncertainty and fear,
mouth words like "don't deserve",
"not good enough" and "waste of space"

So I must get up,
draw back the curtains,
make a mug of tea.

For in the light of day
the demons start to fade,
go back behind closed doors,
leave me in peace.

I can start my day again.

My Holiday

Is there anything more satisfying
than a full English breakfast
with a pot of Yorkshire tea
served in your favourite tea room

then a walk on the prom
and a seat on a bench
looking out to sea.

Someone asked me
where I would like
to go for a holiday.

"Where could I go" I said
"which is better than here?"

The Dog in the Window

I see him most days,
the dog in the window.

For months I thought he was real
until one day he developed a tilt
and I realised the dog was stuffed.

Ownership

Walk round to the prom,
discover two people
are sitting on
my favourite bench.

Feel an irrational
twinge of irritation.
It is not, after all, MY bench.
They are as entitled
to sit there as I am.

Bastards!

Old Fashioned

I sit and stare at my mobile phone,
having just received a text
from a friend in Cuba,
and wonder how that works,
not having a clue.

I see the ads on TV
listing the capabilities
of the latest devices –
waft them over a terminal to pay for goods,
waft them over a picture in the paper to order goods,
watch a film whilst travelling,
read a book on the screen.

Well sorry,
call me old fashioned if you like,
but I prefer –
to see the goods in a shop before I buy,
to pay using actual cash,
to watch the scenery whilst travelling,
and to turn off all electronic devices
before I settle down in my armchair
to read a good book.

It's a Gender Thing

"I have made you a list"
she said
"the top two items
need done today,
the rest need done
yesterday."

He took the list,
read it through carefully,
set it down on the table,
poured himself another cup of tea,
picked up his paper,
said "It'll get done."

Act As If

"Will you stop pretending
you are a student".
she said
"and start pretending
you are a nurse."

So I did.
And somewhere along the line
I decided,
as I was only pretending
to be a nurse
I might as well pretend
to be a good nurse.

I used explain this to patients
and suggest to them
that they could help
by pretending to get well.

And often they did.
And often they did get well.

Somewhere further down the line
I decided I wanted to write poetry.
So I pretended I was a poet,
pretended what I wrote was poetry.

And it seemed like a good idea
to do some more study
so I could pretend
what I wrote
was good poetry.

And often people liked my poetry.
And often those people became my friends.

Just for today
I am pretending
to be a gentle,
compassionate human being
for it is true that

if my reality
is an illusion
which I create for myself
then
I owe it to myself
to create an illusion
which is useful to me.

Memories

It is I have discovered,
looking back, the small stuff
which makes a difference.

Memories of holding hands,
of looking out to sea
watching gannets in formation,
rollers breaking on the shore.

Random, scattered, memories of my two sons,
of my mother, sadly gone,
and of her pride
in each of her four sons.

Memories of making love,
of lying afterwards
talking intimately, gently,
about absolutely nothing.

Memories of laughter,
of skimming stones,
of playing football
on a beach.

The more I look for memories
the more of them I find.
This world is not such a bad place.

Don't Take Yourself Too Seriously

"Don't take yourself too seriously"
she said
"You are not that important."

I was upset at the time.
"How dare she" I thought
for I was taking myself too seriously.

Twenty six and some years later
I can still hear her voice in my head
when I am taking myself too seriously.

And it is true I have found
the more seriously I take myself
the less chance I have of success.

The cure for taking myself too seriously
is my ability to laugh at myself.
The purpose of life, perhaps, is laughter.

Thought for the Day

You never know
when you try
something new
for the first time
whether or not
it is going to work.

But that is never
a good reason
not to try.

The Wind is Blowing a Hooligan

It is raining, snowing, sleeting
long slanting lines which blur
the lights of the town
as they glow dully through the haze.

Two Victorian shelters on
the West Cliff already battered
into submission and distributed
in pieces on the promenade.

The sea, egged on by the wind,
attacks both piers voraciously,
swallows them at times, blows
foam up around the bandstand.

Beyond Captain Cook a figure
appears, well rugged up to be fair,
against the elements, but
seeming fragile nonetheless.

She stands defiantly, struggling
to keep herself and her camera
steady, determined that she will
capture the wildness of the storm.

Windy Corner Tea-room

Where you can get
a delicious Sunday lunch
made just the way
your mother used to make it.

And just like your mother did
Carol will tell you off
if you don't eat up
all your vegetables.

Debonair

I search through my cupboard,
dig out my woolly hat,
for it is that time of year again,
try it on in front of the mirror,
decide I look like Benny from Crossroads.

Do I care? Not really
for surely few people
will remember that character.

And in any event
I have reached an age
where warmth of my head
is much more important
than looking debonair.

Not that I think,
no matter what age,
I ever achieved debonair.

Moving Pictures

Strange, is it not,
how pictures on your wall
gradually, with time,
disappear from view.

I decide to move mine round,
give myself new perspectives
for my days.

I consider each of them in turn
for all of them evoke memories;
one memory leading on to another
as I allow my mind to wander
down those paths, relive again,
sometimes pain, sometimes pleasure,
and I find I can trace
patterns through my life.

Meanwhile the pictures on my wall
remain unmoved but I can
see them once again.

Reach Out

She asks where comes from inspiration for a poem
From a seagull, atop an updraft, motionless
Poems I say are in the air, you have to catch them

From a lapwing's peewit cry echoing in mist
From making love in a car deep in the forest
She asks where do I find the makings of a poem

From conversation overheard in a tearoom
From the deep purple colour of heather in bloom
Open your eyes I say, you just have to catch them

From Atlantic waves breaking on an Irish strand
From a set of footprints embedded in the sand
She asks is that where I can find myself a poem

From glistening lights off beach huts at a sunrise
From the hint of a smile which appears in your eyes
Poems I say are everywhere, you have to grasp them

From our making love, most of all its gentleness
From our lying together after in stillness
Just now she says I caught a glimpse, was that a poem
Poems I say are here with us, reach out and touch them

It's a Man Thing

Get new television
Disconnect old television
Connect new television
Switch it on
Doesn't bloody work

Check all connections
Doesn't bloody work

Switch off TV
Switch off Sky box
Switch on TV
Switch on Sky box
Doesn't bloody work

Re-connect old television
It works
Re-connect new television
Doesn't bloody work

Become increasingly frustrated

Get out instruction booklet
Read it through carefully
Follow instructions

Now it bloody works

2015

It is easy is it not
to become embroiled
in the small things –
the stresses and strains,
the struggles which make up
everyday life.

But looking back
over 2015
the big things
outweigh all the rest.
I have had a good year.

January

I open my curtains this morning.
It has stopped raining
but by the time I pour my second mug of tea
it has started again.

So far this month has provided us
with only fifty shades of grey.

There is a book with that title
but I suspect it has little to do
with Yorkshire in January.

Daily Pleasures

I draw back my curtains,
look out to see
a smattering of snow on grass,
sun gradually cresting
roof tops opposite,
seagulls gathering there
and I smile.

Later I will go round to the prom,
watch sea rolling up the beach,
breaking against walls of the pier
and I will smile again.

There is beauty
in those things
which daily seen
bring pleasure daily.

The Magic

You came for me
from deep in my past,
prompted perhaps
by a poem
I had posted on the Web.

You had changed.
I had changed.
How could we not
after all these years.

Yet we soon discovered
what was between us then
is still between us now.

The magic never dies.

Confusion

Sitting in Windy Corner tea room
with a pot of Yorkshire tea
I find myself
filling salt and pepper pots
whilst Carol and Gail
explain to me
that salt is male
and pepper is female
because it is hot.

I can confuse myself
very well on my own
but being in Windy Corner
accelerates the process.

Wisdom Comes With Age Perhaps

I well remember the times
when I would allow
those who do not matter
to hurt or upset me.

"Pray for the bastards"
I was told
but I could only ever
do that
through gritted teeth.

"Don't let the bastards
live rent free in your head"
I was told
but they would often live on
for days or weeks or months.

Nowadays when insult is aimed
from those who do not matter
I consider allowing myself
to become hurt or upset
and then decide
I really can't be arsed.

Chance Encounter

On my way into town
I stop off at Beckett's
for a mug of coffee
and a toasted teacake
with too much butter.

I get talking, as you do,
with a man
I have never met before.
He asks me
where I am going.

I say I am going
up the east side
to visit a gallery.
I want to see pictures
by a friend of mine.

Turns out his partner
runs that gallery.
He tells me it is closed today.
Saves me a journey.

You can't make this stuff up.

Getting Through My Days

Whilst running the cold tap
in order to rinse away all the suds
after washing the dishes
and before going out
(I have to do that else
the world may come to an end)
and resisting the urge to go for a wee
brought on less by necessity
and more by the sound of running water
I ponder the quirks of behaviour
which help me get through my days.

Go out and lock my front door,
step back a pace, step forward again
and check the door is locked.

Do not drink tea out of a mug designated for coffee
nor coffee out of a mug designated for tea.

Never, ever scour the mug I use
for my early morning tea.
I have had it for years.
"Beyond Therapy" it says on the side.

Lists

Nowadays, more than ever,
I need lists
for there is a difference
between me deciding to do something
and me remembering to do it.

To do lists
Shopping lists
Reminder lists
Daily-Activity lists
May-do-someday lists

There is a list
above my bathroom mirror –
two items on it –
"Your name is David"
"You are OK"

One thing I know for sure –
If it doesn't get written
on a list
it will never get done.

A Gentle Life

Catch the bus up to Windy Corner,
buy a newspaper,
go next door to the tearoom,
join friends at a table,
have breakfast –
bacon, egg and chips
with a large pot of Yorkshire tea.
(Carol joins us for a cup)
Enjoy the company.

Walk back down the prom,
sit awhile, watch the sea,
do the crossword in my paper,
people watch.

Back home, feet up
on the sofa,
read my paper,
watch a football game on TV
(the right team wins)
Settle down for the evening
with a good book.

I am content.

Where Do They Go To In Winter?

Despite the greyness of the day
I am aware that Spring is here
for the gulls have gathered
on the rooftops
preparing for the activities
which form the rituals
of procreation.

Courting
Nesting
Crying raucously
Squabbling
Fighting
That other f word.

I can find myself entertained
as I watch the process unfold
but I do wish they would refrain

from playing havoc
with the plants on my patio,
tapping with their beaks
loudly on my window
and shitting on my car.

Bloody Men

"It'll get done" he said
"But when?" she asked
"Whenever it gets done" he replied
"I am impatient you know
I want it done now"
she said whilst
stamping her feet
and curling her lower lip
"It'll get done" he said

And it did get done
but by that time
she had long since
stormed off into the sunset
chuntering about
"Bloody Men"

Easter Egg

I study the Easter egg
in fancy packaging
on my worktop,
knowing that if I
don't open the packet
I will be able to resist.

But it is an Easter egg
and it is Easter Day.
Would be rude not to.

Wisdom

I have been waiting
for years now
for the wisdom
which is supposed
to come with age.

Guess I will just
have to wait
a bit longer.

God's Will

I sit and ponder
how I got from there to here.

And it does not matter
which there I start from
the pattern remains the same –

Because I did this
that occurred and
because that occurred
some thing else happened.

When I try to combine
because trails the
whole thing gets complicated.

And, of course, I am affected
by the because trails of others –
Because she read one of my poems
and because the poem spoke to her
she got in touch and.........

It could seem that my life
is a series of accidents,
consequences which just happened.

And all I could do
was the best I could do
with the knowledge
I had at the time.

Yet I am aware too
that intent plays its part
in weaving the tapestry of life.

I first fell in love with Whitby
some thirty years ago
and today I am living there.

I ask
"What is God's will for me?"
"See what happens next" she replies
"That will be it."

Days

Yesterday the sun was shining
Today the rain is raining

Yesterday I put away my winter coat
Today I got it out again

Yesterday I walked down the prom
did my crossword
sat on a bench
looking out to sea
Today I drove to the prom
did my crossword
sat in my car
looking out to sea

Yesterday I could see the far horizon
Today I can see only mist
but I can hear the waves

The days will be what the days will be
but the sight and the sound and the smell
of the sea will always calm my soul.

Favourite Bench

I walk round to the prom,
Discover my favourite bench
has vanished, disappeared.

I stand, look around,
check my memory
just in case the bench
existed only in
my imagination.
But I know it was not,
I have written poems about that bench.

I walk closer, discover
the concrete base is still in place,
it is just the bench which is gone,
blown away, taken by the Council, who knows.

I am vaguely disorientated,
have spent almost a year
nurturing that bench.

Somehow the thought of change,
of having to find a new bench,
becomes threatening.

Lament for a Lost Bum

I used to have an attractive bum,
people would comment on it,
refer to it approvingly,
run their hands across it
from time to time in a caress.

Now the thing about bums
is that you cannot see your own,
so it is difficult
to form an objective opinion.

On the eve of his wedding
when I was sharing a room
with my son he referred to it
in disparaging terms.

I no longer have
the same confidence
in my bum
which fuelled my younger days.

Happiness

Happiness comes unexpectedly
as I sit on a bench,
watch a dog race
back and forward on the beach,
chase a ball, catch it,
bring it back, bark for it
to be thrown again,
race off after it.
Meanwhile the other dog
of the pair sits quietly, looks on.

As I watch I equate myself
with the on-looking dog,
yet remember when,
in my younger days,
I would kick a ball
for hours on a beach.

I watch them for ages
then realise,
as I stand up to leave,
I have a smile on my face.

Hugs

It seems to me, looking back,
that in my early years
hugs were in short supply,
not a normal part
of human interaction.

Yet as we progressed
through the sixties
they became an accepted
part of who we were.
Men could hug men,
women hug men,
men and women hug each other,
women could hug children,
men could hug children.

It was, in my experience,
OK for nurses to hug patients.
In fact sometimes that was often
what patients needed most;
just to be hugged, to be held,
for it was the most necessary
part of reassurance.

Now, it seems, that fear
is driving hugs out of existence.
Do I dare hug a female child
who has fallen off her bicycle?

Guilty Pleasures

I am OK
as long as the lid
remains on the tin.

I do not buy biscuits
but strangely sometimes,
when I return from shopping,
I find chocolate hobnobs in my bag.

I put them away,
hide them from myself,
in a tall circular tin
which once held
Cadbury's biscuits.

They cannot call to me
from inside the tin
like they do when
the packet is opened
and in the cupboard.

If you call at my home
for a coffee and a chat
I will offer you
a chocolate biscuit.

You must accept
for it gives me
the opportunity
to open up the tin.

Living in a Cloud

I walk down the prom
as far as Clara's,
call in for a coffee.

A man asks what time is high tide.
Zara does not know, asks me.
I do not know either
so she looks it up on her mobile phone.

Later, whilst sitting outside
drinking my coffee,
I realise the tide
is at its lowest ebb.
Therefore I could have added
six hours and got
an approximate for high tide.

How come, I thought,
I have walked
all that way
along the prom
and never noticed.

Some days I am
so wrapped up
inside my own head
the beauty and mundane
which is present all around me
just passes me by.

For goodness sake, I think,
pay attention.

Brief Encounter 2

I am standing outside the bank
getting money from their machine
when I am approached
by an attractive young lady
who smiles, says hello,
asks me how I am.

Whitby is like that,
people are friendly,
always willing to chat
but it would not be normal
for me to be approached
by a young woman who is a stranger.

I do know her
but from where and from when.
We do chat but I am
too embarrassed to ask.

Nonetheless,
when I leave the bank,
I am smiling.

Growing Older

Life changes as we grow older
and more of us grow older now
than did in the past.

I have reached an age
where I am as likely
to hear about a death
as I am a birthday.

I think about birthdays;
how they mattered when
we were very young,
how thirteen was important –
the start of teenage years,
how sixteen was important –
the age of legitimate sex lives,
how eighteen was important –
legal then to go into pubs,
how twenty one was important
although I am not sure why.

In our middle years birthdays
become less significant
except perhaps for those
with a zero on the end.

But now, when I hear about death,
birthdays acquire a new significance,
each one a cause for celebration,
a fist pump, a see-I-made-it smile.

But I do not plan for my next one,
too much like tempting fate,
although I have booked tickets
to see an Elvis-on-the-big-screen concert
two months after my next birthday.

Guess I plan to live that long.

Lorraine

We visited the hospital together.
Either she was providing support for me
as I had a hospital appointment
or I was providing support for her
as she had a hospital appointment.
I cannot now remember which.

After, we needed a rest,
a chance to reflect on how we felt,
so went for a coffee
in the coffee shop in the hospital,
bloody awful coffee,
but it was somewhere to sit.

She admired the menus,
remarked on the colours,
said she could make jewellery from them.
So when we left I took with me
a number of menus hidden in my paper.

She made beads from the menus,
strung some of them together
to make a bracelet,
gave it to me as a present.

I have worn it every day since.

Clara’s

I sit at Clara’s
sheltered from the wind
in the seating area
Chris has built at the back;
rain is spotting on my head
but not enough to make me wet.

My doctor tells me
I need to exercise more;
I don’t suppose
lifting a coffee cup
up to my mouth
really counts.

Gail

I walk into Windy Corner
for my brunch.
I do that most days
for it saves me cooking.

I ask for
what I think I want.
Gail serves me with
what she thinks I want.

Some days it is easier
just to ask
“What am I having today?”

Old Songs

"The sun is out,
the sky is blue,
there's not a cloud
to spoil the view"

An old song pops into my head
as I pull open the curtains
this morning. An old song which dates
from almost sixty years ago.
It will likely stay in my head
for the remainder of the day.

Is it any wonder I have
difficulty remembering
yesterday. There is no room for
new things, my head is already
full with old songs from yesteryear.

Beckett's

Call in at Beckett's
for a mug of coffee
and a chat.

Congratulate Jess.
She is really, really
pleased with herself.
I am delighted for her.

Julie tells me
she has sold
some more of my books.
A good start to my day.

She goes on to discuss
my diet, wonders how
I have reached my age
without knowing
what is healthy food.

Actually, looking back
on my life
I wonder how I have
reached my age any way.

Every new day is a good day.

Living the Dream

You have to have a dream,
for it is the dream
which will sustain you
in the bad days
when darkness descends
and the dark, it seems,
has no edges.

You have to have a dream,
for it is the dream
which gives you purpose,
drives the hard work
which is necessary
to make the dream come true.

And when you get to live the dream
you must be grateful,
for it is that gratitude
which allows you
to put in the effort
which keeps the dream alive.

www.ingramcontent.com/pod-product-compliance
Ingram Content Group UK Ltd.
Pitfield, Milton Keynes, MK11 3LW, UK
UKHW020236250726
13967UKWH00001B/408